# Making It! Judo Champion

Eleanor Archer

FRANKLIN WATTS
NEW YORK • LONDON • SYDNEY

Ian is a judo champion. He competes in judo competitions all over the world.

Ian is blind. He can see a little but everything is blurred. Only a few people who are blind see nothing at all.

The photo above shows Ian's wife, Debbie and his daughter, Leah.

This is how Ian sees them from a distance.

On Saturday, Ian is taking part in a competition. He needs to be very fit to be a judo champion so today he is going to the gym to work out.

Ian is not allowed to drive. Debbie usually drives Ian where he wants to go. Sometimes he uses trains or buses to travel about.

At the gym Ian signs in at reception. "Good morning!" says Ian. Then he gets changed. First Ian uses a machine that works the muscles in his legs.

Then Ian moves to a different machine. "I need to build up my arm muscles," he thinks to himself. Ian has to be strong enough to throw his opponent in judo.

Steve helps Ian with some of the weight machines. People who are blind will ask for help if they need it.

Before he leaves the gym, Ian has a drink with a friend. "I'm in a competition in Germany on Saturday," he tells him. "Good luck!" says his friend.

If you are chatting to a person who cannot see at all it is important to tell them when you are leaving so they know you are going.

When Ian gets home, he goes for a run. He runs for thirty minutes every day.

Outside, the bright sun makes it harder for Ian to see. "I nearly ran into this car!" he thinks.

Cars or bicycles left on the pavement make it difficult for blind people or people who use wheelchairs to pass by.

Ian runs across a busy road. He looks and listens carefully to make sure no cars or bicycles are coming. Then he crosses safely.

Ian knows where to cross the road because he can feel the bumps on the pavement under his feet.

Later, Ian relaxes at home. He reads a newsletter about the competition. "I'm looking forward to travelling to Germany with the team," he thinks to himself.

Ian uses a magnifying glass to read. It makes the letters bigger so they are easier to see.

Ian telephones a friend who is on the judo team. "The aeroplane leaves at 2.30 p.m. tomorrow," Ian tells Bob. "Don't be late!"

On a touch telephone there is a little bump on the 5. It helps people who are blind to know which numbers they are pressing.

Then Ian packs his bags for the weekend. "Judo kit, toothbrush…" he thinks. He has made a list for himself.

Ian keeps his clothes tidy. It helps him to find something when he needs it.

The next day, Debbie takes Ian to the airport to catch the aeroplane to Germany. "Good luck!" she tells him.

Ian checks in. He gives the attendant his ticket and passport. "That's fine, thank you," says the attendant.

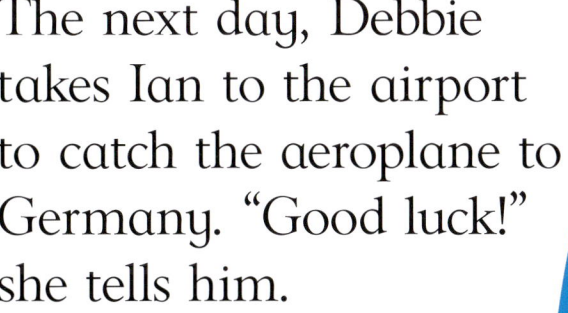

Ian doesn't know the airport very well so Debbie guides him and the luggage trolley.

On the aeroplane the attendant makes sure everything is OK. "Just press the buzzer if you need any help," she tells Ian.

At last, it's competition day! First the competitors are weighed.

When it is Ian's turn to fight, he is led onto the mat.

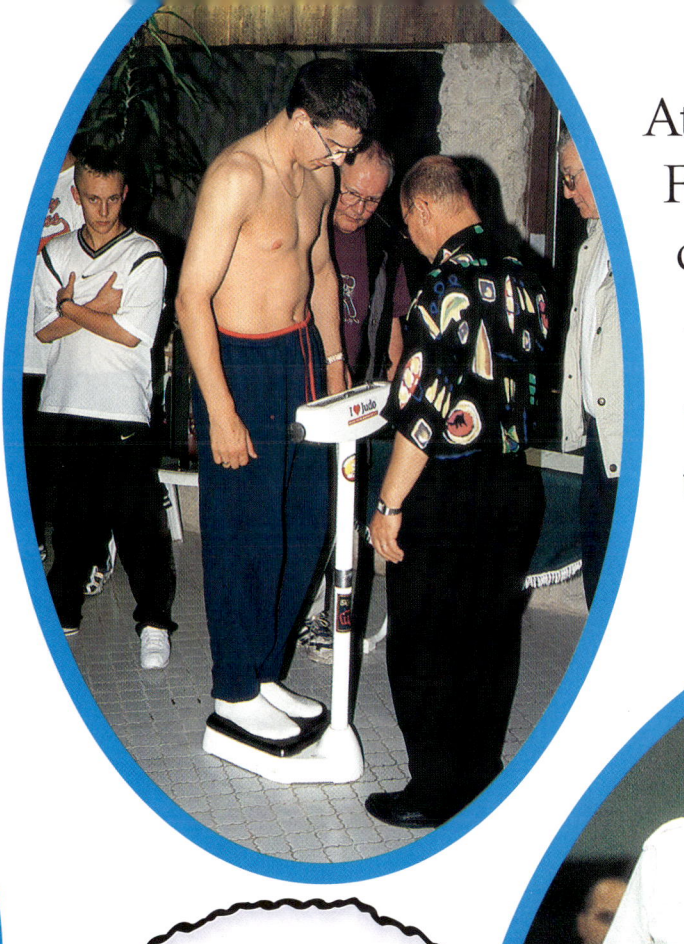

Blind people can do the same things as sighted people, but sometimes do them in different ways. Ian is led to the competition area because he cannot see well enough.

Ian and his opponent face each other and bow. Then the referee says "go" and the fight begins.

Ian throws his opponent onto the mat. He holds him for thirty seconds. Ian has to fight three times.

Ian and his opponent are both blind so they are allowed to touch each other before the fight. Then they know exactly where the other person is standing.

Ian has won all three fights!

At the end, he is led off the mat. "That went really well!" Ian thinks to himself.

Ian wins a gold medal and certificate.
"Brilliant!" says Ian. "I've won!"

# So you want to be a judo champion?

1. Join a local judo club. It takes a lot of practice to become a champion.

2. Start getting fit! You need lots of energy.

3. You will start with a white belt. If you are good enough you can win different coloured belts. They are yellow, orange, green, blue and brown. The top judo champions are black belts.

4. Remember you will be part of a team or squad as well as competing for yourself.

5. Judo is a Japanese sport. Competitions are called fights. The referee starts each fight saying "Hajime," which means "go" in Japanese. At the end of the fight the referee says "Matte" which means "stop".

# Facts about blindness

- Some people are born blind or partially sighted, others lose their sight because of illness or accidents.

- People who don't see very well sometimes need help to get around. Some people use guide dogs. Others have long white canes or they ask a friendly person to show them the way.

- Only a few blind people see nothing at all. Most can tell the difference between light and dark.

- Some blind people use braille to read and write. Braille is a system made up of raised dots arranged in different patterns to make letters. The person reads the braille with their fingers.

# How you can help

- Learn how to guide a person who is blind or cannot see well. Offer the person your arm. Then walk slightly ahead of them so they can tell which direction you are going.

- Offer to help and remember to listen to the blind person's answer. They may be able to manage on their own.

- Touch a blind person on the shoulder and say who you are when you first speak. It is not always possible to recognise a person from their voice.

- If you see a guide dog leading a blind person, do not make a fuss of the dog, it's working!

# Addresses and further information

**The Royal National Institute for the Blind (RNIB)**
Helpline 0845 766 999
Information, support and advice for anyone with a serious sight problem.
http:\\www.rnib.org.uk

**British Blind Sports**
4-6 Victoria Street
Leamington Spa CV31 3AB

**REACH National Advice Centre for Children with Reading Difficulties**
Nine Mile Ride
California Country Park
Finchampstead, RG40 4HT

**Royal Blind Society**
4 Mitchell Road
Enfield
NSW 2136 Sydney
Australia

# Index

aeroplane 11, 13, 14

airport 13

blind 3, 6, 8, 11, 15, 16, 17

competition 2, 4, 7, 10, 15

crossing the road 9

driving 4

Germany 7, 10, 13

gold medal 19

guiding 13, 22

magnifying glass 10

opponent 6, 16, 17

pavements 8, 9

reading 10

running 8, 9

telephone 11

tidy 12

working out 4, 5, 6

© 2000 Franklin Watts

Franklin Watts
96 Leonard Street
London
EC2A 4XD

Franklin Watts Australia
14 Mars Road
Lane Cove
NSW 2066

ISBN: 0 7496 3665 3

Dewey Decimal Classification Number: 362.4

10 9 8 7 6 5 4 3 2 1

A CIP catalogue record for this book is available from the British Library.

Printed in Malaysia

**Consultants:** Bernard Fleming/Charles Gainsford, RNIB; Beverley Mathias, REACH.
**Editor:** Samantha Armstrong
**Designer:** Louise Snowdon
**Photographers:** Bob Willingham (cover, P2, P13-19); All others by Chris Fairclough
**Illustrator:** Derek Matthews

**With thanks to:** Ian, Debbie and Leah Rose, Bodyfit Gym, High Wycombe and British Blind Sports.